Twenty to

Knitted
Snoods

Monica Russel

Search Press

First published in 2016

Search Press Limited
Wellwood, North Farm Road,
Tunbridge Wells, Kent TN2 3DR

Text copyright © Monica Russel 2016

Photographs by Garie Hind
Photograph on page 8 by Paul Bricknell

Photographs and design copyright
© Search Press Ltd 2016

Print ISBN: 978-1-78221-322-2
ebook ISBN: 978-1-78126-354-9

The Publishers and author can accept no
responsibility for any consequences arising from
the information, advice or instructions given in
this publication.

Readers are permitted to reproduce any of the
items in this book for their personal use, or for
the purposes of selling for charity, free of
charge and without the prior permission of the
Publishers. Any use of the items for commercial
purposes is not permitted without the prior
permission of the Publishers.

Suppliers
If you have difficulty in obtaining any of the
materials and equipment mentioned in this
book, then please visit the Search Press website
for details of suppliers: www.searchpress.com

Printed in China

Dedication
To Trevor, Claerwen and my sons Jacob
and Matthew for their continuous support,
encouragement and patience whilst I knit
and design. Also a huge thank you to
Jeannine for trying on my samples.

Acknowledgements
Without help from Chas and Rachel at
UK Alpaca, and Pete and John from
Rooster Yarns, I would not have had the
opportunity to use such a variety and colour
range of yarns for the projects in this book.
I really appreciate the specialist yarns
donated by Beverley from The Handspinner
Having Fun, Jeni at Fyberspates, Susan from
Yarn Garden, Susan and Karen at Mrs Moon,
Linda at Tall Yarns, Julie from Watercolours &
Lace, and Sara at Sara's Texture Crafts.
They have helped me enormously to
expand my choices of natural fibres.
Finally, a huge thank you to
Katie French for commissioning this book,
to May Corfield, my editor, Mary Ellingham,
publicity manager, and to the team at
Search Press for their invaluable
encouragement and support. For the
purchase of yarns and other patterns,
please visit the author's website:
www.theknitknacks.co.uk

Contents

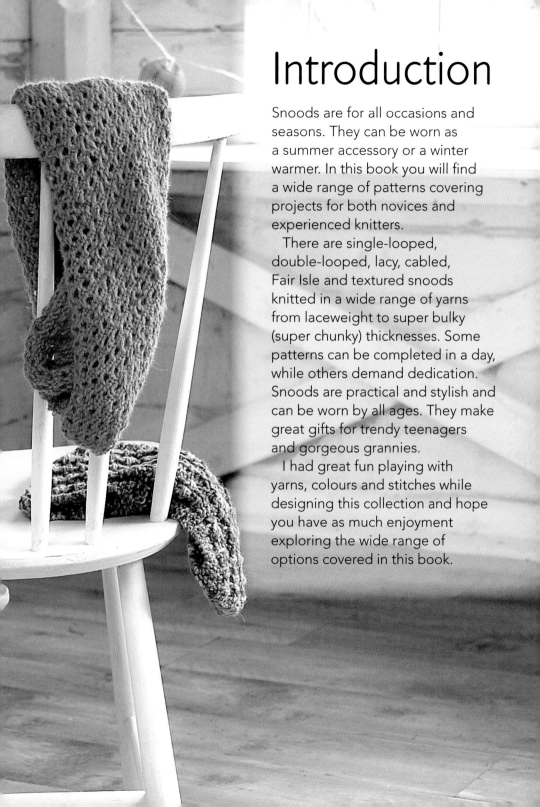

Introduction

Snoods are for all occasions and seasons. They can be worn as a summer accessory or a winter warmer. In this book you will find a wide range of patterns covering projects for both novices and experienced knitters.

There are single-looped, double-looped, lacy, cabled, Fair Isle and textured snoods knitted in a wide range of yarns from laceweight to super bulky (super chunky) thicknesses. Some patterns can be completed in a day, while others demand dedication. Snoods are practical and stylish and can be worn by all ages. They make great gifts for trendy teenagers and gorgeous grannies.

I had great fun playing with yarns, colours and stitches while designing this collection and hope you have as much enjoyment exploring the wide range of options covered in this book.

Knitting know-how

General notes

These snoods will make either a single or a double wrap depending on the length given. The lengths are for guidance and can be adapted to suit individual measurements. If you want to extend the shorter snoods you will require extra yarn.

Yarn

Most yarn today comes in ready-prepared balls or skeins. These come in different weights and thicknesses and you can knit directly from them. Other yarn comes in hanks, which are big loops of yarn that are bought by weight and thickness. Before knitting, they need to be wound into a ball so that the yarn does not get knotted as you work.

There are a variety of yarns used in the snood projects and these can be substituted for those of your choice. It is advisable to check the length and weight of yarn that you buy against the ones used in the patterns to ensure that you have enough to finish your projects.

Laceweight (1–3 ply) yarn is a very fine yarn that is used for more open patterns. Generally, you get very long yardage in a 50g ball or hank. Sometimes lighter weight yarns can be doubled to create a more dense look.

Light worsted (DK/8-ply) yarn is a medium thickness yarn that is suitable for many projects. The main light worsted (DK/8-ply) yarn used in these projects is made from alpaca wool, with each ball containing 131yd (120m) of yarn.

Worsted (aran/10-ply) yarn is thicker than light worsted (DK/8-ply) yarn and will produce correspondingly thicker snoods.

Bulky (chunky) yarn is thicker still and will produce lovely, snuggly snoods that are ideal for cold weather.

See opposite for details of the actual yarns used for the projects in this book.

For a list of knitting abbreviations, see the table on page 48.

Needles

Needles made from sustainable wood were used for all the projects. I enjoy knitting with them because of their durability, and they are flexible to work with in all temperatures.

For some of the projects I used cable needles; these were also made from sustainable wood and I find that the yarns stay on them better than the metal or plastic ones.

Other materials

For all the projects you will need a pair of good-quality, sharp scissors to snip off loose ends of yarn after weaving them into your work.

As well as knitting needles, you will also need a blunt-ended needle with a large eye, such as a tapestry needle, for sewing up all your projects and weaving in any loose ends.

Mattress stitch

Mattress stitch makes a practically invisible and nicely flexible seam for joining pieces together.

1 With the right sides of the work facing, start with your yarn in the lower right corner. Take your tapestry needle across to the left edge and under the strand of yarn between the first and second stitches of the first row.

2 Take your needle back to the right edge and insert it one row up, between the first and second stitches of the row.

3 Take your needle back to the left edge and repeat steps one and two.

4 After completing a few stitches, gently pull the long end of the yarn to draw the stitches together and 'fuse' the two pieces of knitting so that the join is invisible.

Cable cast-on

This technique is used in patterns where you need to cast on in the middle of a row.

Insert your knitting needle between the first two stitches, wrap the yarn round the needle and bring it through to the front of your work. Transfer the newly created stitch onto the left-hand needle, thus increasing a stitch.

Tensions/gauges

All the tensions given for the yarns below are the manufacturer's guidelines (except where stated) and for 4 x 4in (10 x 10cm) swatches knitted in stockinette stitch (UK stocking stitch); these will be helpful if you decide to use alternative yarns to those used in the projects.

Yarns

Bulky (chunky)

Mrs Moon Plump: 80% superfine Australian new merino, 20% baby alpaca.

Tension: 10 sts x 12.5 rows using 10mm (US 15/UK 000) needles.

Yardage: 100g/77yd/70m.

Used for Gooseberry Fool snood.

Worsted (aran/10-ply)

Roosters Almerino Aran: 50% baby alpaca, merino wool.

Tension: 19 sts x 23 rows using 5.5mm (US 9, UK 5) needles.

Yardage: 50g/103yd/94m.

Used for Leaf snood.

Fyberspates Scrumptious Aran: 45% silk, 55% merino.

Tension: 18 sts x 24 rows using 5mm (US 8, UK 6) needles.

Yardage: 100g/180yd/165m.

Used for Scrumptious snood.

Sarah's Texture Crafts Superwash Aran: 100% Bluefaced Leicester.

Tension: 17 sts x 22 rows using 5mm (US 8, UK 6) needles.

Yardage: 100g/181yd/166m.

Used for Purple Mist snood.

Light worsted (DK/8-ply)

Roosters Almerino DK: 50% baby alpaca, 50% merino wool.

Tension: 21 sts x 28 rows using 4mm (US 6, UK 8) needles.

Yardage: 50g/124yd/113m.

Used for Rooster and Blossom snoods.

UK Alpaca Superfine Alpaca: 70% alpaca, 30% Bluefaced Leicester.

Tension: 20 sts x 29 rows using 4mm (US 6, UK 8) needles.

Yardage: 50g/131yd/120m.

Used for Matisse, Harlequin and Foxy Boxy snoods.

UK Alpaca Baby: 80% baby alpaca, 20% superfine merino.

Tension: 20 sts x 29 rows using 4mm (US 6, UK 8) needles.

Yardage: 50g/122yd/112m.

Used for Caramel and Graphite snoods.

Fyberspates Vivacious DK: 100% superwash merino wool.

Tension: 22 sts x 28 rows using 4mm (US 6, UK 8) needles.

Yardage: 100g/251yd/230m.

Used for Regal snood.

The Handspinner Having Fun: 100% silk hand-dyed yarn.

Tension over cable pattern: 19 sts x 22 rows using 5mm (US 8, UK 6) needles.

Yardage: 100g/153yd/145m.

Used for Starry Night snood.

Manos del Uruguay Silk Blend DK: 30% silk, 70% extra fine merino.

Tension: 22 sts x 28 rows using 4mm (US 6, UK 8) needles.

Yardage: 50g/150yd/135m.

Used for Heather and Muriel snoods.

Fingering (4-ply)

Watercolours & Lace silk fingering (4-ply): 50% merino wool, 50% silk.

Tension: 48 sts x 28 rows using 3.5mm (US 3, UK 10) needles.

Yardage: 100g/492yd/400m.

Used for Summer Garden and Minty snoods.

Manos del Uruguay 4-ply: 30% silk, 70% wool.

Tension: 24 sts x 30 rows using 4mm (US 6, UK 8) needles.

Yardage: 50g/246yd/225m.

Used for Agincourt snood.

Laceweight (2-ply)

Yarn Garden lace: 65% baby alpaca, 20% silk, 10% cashmere, 5% stellina.

Tension: 16 sts x 17 rows over pattern using 4mm (US 6, UK 8) needles.

Yardage: 100g/984yd/800m.

Used for Adriatic snood.

Roosters Lace: 80% alpaca, 20% silk.

Tension 20–39sts x 33–54 rows using 2mm (US 00, UK 14) needles and 4mm (US 6, UK 8) needles.

Yardage: 100g/874yd/800m.

Used for Ophelia snood.

Scrumptious

Materials:

3 balls of worsted (aran/10-ply) silk/merino yarn – 1 x magenta (A), 1 x green (B) and 1 x purple (C); 100g/180yd/165m

Needles:

5mm (US 8, UK 6) circular knitting needle

6mm (US 10, UK 4) circular knitting needle

1 stitch marker

Size:

Circumference: 29⅛in (74cm), height: 9¾in (25cm)

Tension:

20 sts x 24 rows = 4in (10cm) square using 5mm (US 8, UK 6) needles

												12
												11
												10
												9
												8
												7
												6
												5
												4
												3
												2
												1

12 11 10 9 8 7 6 5 4 3 2 1

Instructions:

Row 1: using 5mm (US 8, UK 6) circular knitting needle and yarn A, cast on 144 sts. Place a stitch marker to denote start of each round. Join the round, being careful not to twist any stitches.

Rounds 1 and 2: *k1, p1, repeat from * to end of round, moving the stitch marker up at the end of each round.

Rounds 3–14: work pattern from chart twisting the yarn every 2–3 sts to avoid large loops at the back of the work.

Repeat the 12-row pattern another three times.

Fasten off yarns B and C.

Work 2 rounds in a 1 x 1 rib as for rounds 1 and 2. Cast off using 6mm (US 10, UK 4) circular knitting needle.

Making up

Press snood lightly. Weave in all loose ends.

This is a snood for all seasons. The vibrant colours and Fair Isle pattern make it stand out from the crowd, but it could also be knitted in soft pastel colours.

Matisse

Materials:

4 balls of light worsted (DK/8-ply) alpaca
yarn – 3 x dark grey (A), 1 x mustard (B);
50g/131yd/120m

Needles:

4mm (US 6, UK 8) knitting needles

Size:

Circumference 29½in (75cm),
height: 12¼in (31cm)

Tension:

19 sts x 26 rows = 4in (10cm) square
using 4mm (US 6, UK 8) needles

Instructions:

Using yarn A, cast on 64 sts.

Foundation row: knit each st tbl to form a neat edge.

Row 1: (RS) knit.

Row 2: k3, purl to last 3 sts, k3.

Continue this two-row pattern until work measures 29½in
(75cm) ending with a WS row.

Fasten off yarn A.

Using yarn B, work picot method cast-off as follows:

Next row: k2, cast off 2 sts, * transfer st on right needle
to left-hand needle and cast on 2 sts using cable cast on,
cast off 4 sts, repeat from * to end of row.

Making up

Press snood lightly. Join ends using yarn B, slightly
gathering the picot edge so it matches the cast-on edge.
Weave in all loose ends.

*This is a very simple snood that
is quick to knit. It has a stylish
edge in a contrasting colour
that gives it a certain panache.*

Summer Garden

Materials:

2 balls of fingering (4-ply) merino/silk yarn in variegated blue/lilac; 100g/437yd/400m

4 buttons of choice

Needles:

3.5mm (US 4, UK 10) knitting needles

Size:

Circumference: 49½in (126cm), height: 9in (23cm)

Tension:

34 sts x 27 rows = 4in (10cm) square over pattern using 3.5mm (US 4, UK 10) needles

Instructions:

Cast on 78 sts.

Foundation row: knit each st tbl to form a neat edge.

Row 1: (RS) k3, *sl 1, k2tog, psso, k7, yfwd, k1, yfrn, p2, yon, k1, yfwd, k7, k3tog, rep from * twice more, k3.

Row 2 and every alternate row: k3, *p11, k2, p11, rep from * twice more, k3.

Row 3: k3, *sl 1, k2tog, psso, k6, (yfwd, k1) twice, p2, (k1, yfwd) twice, k6, k3tog, rep from * twice more, k3.

Row 5: k3, *sl 1, k2tog, psso, k5, yfwd, k1, yfwd, k2, p2, k2, yfwd, k1, yfwd, k5, k3tog, rep from * twice more, k3.

Row 7: k3, *sl 1, k2tog, psso, k4, yfwd, k1, yfwd, k3, p2, k3, yfwd, k1, yfwd, k4, k3tog, rep from * twice more, k3.

Row 9: k3, *s1, k2tog, psso, k3, yfwd, k1, yfwd, k4, p2, k4, yfwd, k1, yfwd, k3, k3tog, rep from * twice more, k3.

Row 10: as row 2.

Repeat this 10-row pattern until work measures approximately 49½in (126cm) ending with a row 10.

Cast off, leaving a long yarn tail for sewing up your work.

Making up

Press snood lightly. Sew on buttons in the centre of the four scallops. Overlap the scalloped edges on the back of the snood and sew into place. Weave in all loose ends.

This is a very pretty spring or summer snood knitted in a lace pattern that highlights the variegated but muted colour of the yarn. The snood is worn by wrapping it twice round your neck.

Regal

Materials:

2 balls of light worsted (DK/8-ply) merino wool in two shades of green; 100g/251yd/230m

Needles:

6.5mm (US 10.5, UK 3) circular knitting needle

1 stitch marker

Size:

Circumference: 26³⁄₈in (67cm), height: 9½in (24cm)

Tension:

11.5 sts x 25 rows = 4in (10cm) square using 6.5mm (US 10.5, UK 3) needles with yarn doubled

Instructions:

Note: the yarn is held double throughout this pattern.

Cast on 77 sts. Place a stitch marker to denote start of each round. Join the round, being careful not to twist any stitches.

Round 1: *k1, p1, rep from * to last st, k1.

Round 2: *p1, k1, rep from * to last st, p1.

Repeat these 2 rounds until work measures approximately 9½in (24cm) in height.

Cast off.

Making up

Press snood lightly. Weave in all loose ends.

This simple snood is knitted in moss stitch using a luxurious yarn that blends two colours together. It is knitted in the round and is very quick to make.

Rooster

Materials:

4 balls of light worsted (DK/8-ply) alpaca/
merino yarn – 1 x gooseberry (A), 1 x
damson (B), 1 x red (C) and 1 x cream (D);
50g/124yd/113m

Needles:

4.5mm (US 7, UK 7) circular knitting needle

1 stitch marker

Size:

Circumference: 26in (66cm), height: 10¼in (26cm)

Tension:

23 sts x 29 rows = 4in (10cm) over Fair Isle using
4.5mm (US 7, UK 7) needles

Instructions:

Using yarn A, cast on 150 sts. Place a stitch
marker to denote start of each round. Join the
round, being careful not to twist any stitches.

Rounds 1 and 2: knit in A.

Round 3: *k2B, k1A, rep from * to end of round.

Rounds 4 and 5: *k2A, k1B, rep from * to end
of round.

Round 6: *k2B, k1A, rep from * to end of round.

Rounds 7 and 8: knit in A.

Fasten off yarns A and B.

Rounds 9 and 10: using yarn C, knit.

Round 11: *k2D, k3C, rep from * to end
of round.

Rounds 12 and 13: k3D, *k1C, k4D, rep from
* to last 2 sts, k1C, k1D.

Round 14: *k2D, k3C, rep from * to end
of round.

Rounds 15 and 16: knit in C.

Rounds 17–24: work as rounds 1–8, reversing
the yarn colours.

Rounds 25–32: work as rounds 9–16.

Work rounds 1–32 once more.

Rounds 65–72: work as rounds 1–8.

Cast off in A.

Making up

Press snood lightly. Weave in all loose ends.

*How lovely it is to find a great yarn in
colours that contrast, yet blend together
so well. This simple Fair Isle snood
works by using combinations of colours
that are interchangeable. The snood is
knitted in the round.*

Heather

Materials:
4 balls of light worsted (DK/8-ply) silk/merino yarn in variegated purple; 50g/150yd/135m

Needles:
4.5mm (US 7, UK 7) circular knitting needle

1 stitch marker

Size:
Circumference: 57in (144cm), height: 9½in (24cm)

Tension:
18 sts x 32 rows = 4in (10cm) square using 4.5mm (US 7, UK 7) needles

Instructions:

Cast on 264 sts. Place a stitch marker to denote start of each round. Join the round, being careful not to twist any stitches.

Rounds 1 and 2: *k1, p1, rep from * to end of round.

Round 3: *p1, k1, rep from * to end of round.

Round 4: *k1, p1, rep from * to end of round.

Rounds 5 and 6: as rounds 3 and 4.

Eyelet textured section (pattern repeat of 22 sts):

Round 1: *(k1, p1) three times, (yo, k2tog, k2) four times, rep from * to end of round.

Round 2: *(p1, k1) three times, k16, rep from * to end of round.

Round 3: *(k1, p1) three times, (k2, yo, k2tog) four times, rep from * to end of round.

Round 4: as round 2.

Repeat these 4 rounds six more times, then repeat rounds 1–3 once more.

Knit 6 rounds.

Next round: *(p1, k1) three times, k16, rep from * to end of round.

Next round: *(k1, p1) three times, k16, rep from * to end of round.

Next round: *(p1, k1) three times, k15, MB in next stitch, rep from * to end of round.

Next round: *(k1, p1) three times, k16, rep from * to end of round.

Next round: *(p1, k1) three times, k16, rep from * to end of round.

Knit 6 rounds.

Now work rounds 1–4 of eyelet textured rounds seven times, then repeat rounds 1–3 once more.

Next round: *k1, p1, rep from * to end of round.

Next round: *p1, k1, rep from * to end of round.

Repeat the last 2 rounds once more.

Next 2 rounds: *p1, k1, rep from * to end of round.

Cast off.

Making up
Press snood lightly. Weave in all loose ends.

This snood embraces a mix of moss stitch and a very simple lace pattern. It is knitted in a variegated silky yarn that is light to wear throughout the year. It is one of a selection in the book that is knitted in the round.

Gooseberry Fool

Materials:

3 balls of bulky (chunky) merino/baby alpaca yarn – 2 x dark grey (A), 1 x green (B); 100g/87yd/70m

Needles:

10mm (US 15, UK 000) knitting needles

Size:

Circumference: 51in (130cm), height: 10in (25cm)

Tension:

8 sts x 14 rows = 4in (10cm) square using 10mm (US 15, UK 000) needles

Instructions:

Using yarn A, cast on 21 sts.

Foundation row: knit each st tbl to form a neat edge.

Rows 1–6: using yarn A, *k1, k2tog, rep from * to end.

Rows 7–10: using yarn B, knit.

Repeat these 10 rows until work measures approximately 51¼in (130cm) ending with row 10.

Cast off, leaving a long yarn tail for sewing up your work.

Making up

Press snood lightly. Join cast-on and cast-off ends using mattress stitch with RS facing. Weave in all loose ends.

This is a great quick knit and a very simple pattern that an almost novice knitter could make. I have used a bulky (chunky) lightweight yarn that drapes beautifully.

Starry Night

Materials:
3 balls of light worsted (DK/8-ply) mulberry silk
  yarn; 100g/153yd/140m

Needles:
5mm (US 8, UK 6) knitting needles

1 x cable needle

Size:
Circumference: 50½in (128cm), height: 9in (23cm)

Tension:
19 sts x 22 rows = 4in (10cm) square using 5mm
  (US 8, UK 6) needles

Instructions:
Cast on 44 sts.

Foundation row: knit each st tbl to form a
neat edge.

Row 1: k11, p3, k2, p4, k4, p4, k2, p3, k11.

Row 2 and all even-numbered rows: k11, work
each of the next 22 sts as it appears on this side
of the work (knit the k sts and purl the p sts), k11.

Row 3: k11, p3, k2, p4, C4B, p4, k2, p3, k11.

Row 5: k11, p3, T3F, p2, T3B, T3F, p2, T3B,
p3, k11.

Row 7: k11, p4, T3F, T3B, p2, T3F, T3B, p4, k11.

Row 9: k11, p5, C4B, p4, C4B, p5, k11.

Row 11: k11, p5, k4, p4, k4, p5, k11.

Row 13: as row 9.

Row 15: k11, p4, T3B, T3F, p2, T3B, T3F,
p4, k11.

Row 17: k11, p3, T3B, p2, T3F, T3B, p2, T3F,
p3, k11.

Row 19: as row 3.

Repeat rows 1–20 until work measures
approximately 50½in (128cm).

Cast off, leaving a long yarn tail for sewing up
your work.

Making up

Press snood lightly. Join cast-on and cast-off
ends using mattress stitch with RS facing.
Weave in all loose ends.

*This snood is made from a hand-
dyed silk that gives it a wonderful
rich colour and sheen, highlighted
by the raised cable pattern. The
snood can be worn by wrapping it
round the neck twice.*

Graphite

Materials:

8 balls of worsted (aran/10-ply) baby alpaca/
  merino yarn – 1 x light blue (A), 3 x cream (B),
  1 x mint green (C), 1 x turquoise (D), 1 x dark
  blue (E) and 1 x pink (F); 50g/102yd/94m

Needles:

5mm (US 8, UK 6) knitting needles

Size:

Circumference: 58in (148cm),
  height: 11½in (29cm)

Tension:

22 sts x 20 rows = 4in (10cm) square using 5mm
  (US 8, UK 6) needles

Instructions:

Cast on 60 sts using yarn A.

Foundation row: knit each stitch tbl to form a
neat edge.

Row 1: k3A, work row 1 from chart three
times, k3B.

The odd-numbered rows are worked
from right to left and are knitted, the even-
numbered rows are worked from left to right
and are purled.

Continue working from the chart, noting that
the first and last three sts of every row (not
shown on the chart) are knitted in the start and
end colour, to form a g st edge, and the rest of
the work is completed in st st.

Continue until work measures approximately
58in (148cm), finishing with last row of chart.
Cast off, leaving a long yarn tail for sewing up
your work.

Making up

Press snood lightly. Join cast-on and cast-off
ends using mattress stitch with RS facing.
Weave in all loose ends.

Key:

A B C D E F

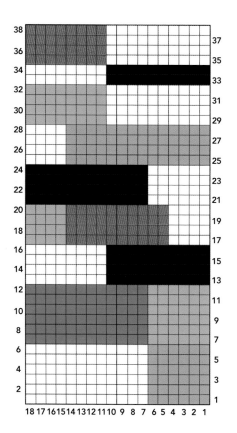

This is a great project for an evening. Simply choose your favourite colours in a soft yarn for a luxurious snood.

Leaf

Materials:

3 balls of worsted (aran/10-ply) baby alpaca/merino yarn; 50g/103yd/94m

Needles:

5.5mm (US 9, UK 5) knitting needles

1 cable needle

Size:

Circumference: 46in (117cm), height: 7½in (19cm)

Tension:

19 sts x 23 rows = 4in (10cm) square using 5.5mm (US 9, UK 5) needles

Instructions:

Cast on 44 sts.

Foundation row: knit each st tbl to form a neat edge.

Note: in order to stop the edges curling, each odd-numbered row starts with p1, k1, p1, k1 and ends with k1, p1, k1, p1.

The even-numbered rows start with k1, p1, k1, p1 and end with p1, k1, p1, k1. These sts are not included in the following instructions.

Pattern is knitted over 32 rows and repeated four times across the row.

Row 1: (RS) C2F, p7.

Row 2: k6, T2FW, p1.

Row 3: KB1, p1, C2F, p5.

Row 4: k4, T2FW, p1, k1, p1.

Row 5: (KB1, p1) twice, C2F, p3.

Row 6: k2, T2FW, (p1, k1) twice, p1.

Row 7: (KB1, p1) three times, C2F, p1.

Row 8: T2FW, (p1, k1) three times, p1.

Row 9: (KB1, p1) four times, KB1.

Row 10: (p1, k1) three times, p1, T2FW.

Row 11: p1, T2F, (p1, KB1) three times.

Row 12: (p1, k1) twice, p1, T2FW, k2.

Row 13: p3, T2F, (p1, KB1) twice.

Row 14: p1, k1, p1, T2FW, k4.

Row 15: p5, T2F, p1, KB1.

Row 16: p1, T2FW, k6.

Row 17: p7, C2B.

Row 18: p1, T2BW, k6.

Row 19: p5, C2B, p1, KB1.

Row 20: p1, k1, p1, T2BW, k4.

Row 21: p3, C2B, (p1, KB1) twice.

Row 22: (p1, k1) twice, p1, T2BW, k2.

Row 23: p1, C2B, (p1, KB1) three times.

Row 24: (p1, k1) three times, p1, T2BW.

Row 25: (KB1, p1) four times, KB1.

Row 26: T2BW, (p1, k1) three times, p1.

Row 27: (KB1, p1) three times, T2B, p1.

Row 28: k2, T2BW, (p1, k1) twice, p1.

Row 29: (KB1, p1) twice, T2B, p3.

Row 30: k4, T2BW, p1, k1, p1.

Row 31: KB1, p1, T2B, p5.

Row 32: k6, T2BW, p1.

Repeat these 32 rows until work measures approximately 46in (117cm).

Cast off, leaving a long yarn tail for sewing up your work.

Making up

Press snood lightly. Join cast-on and cast-off ends using mattress stitch with RS facing. Weave in all loose ends.

This snood is made using a non-traditional cable. I have used a classic colour that will go with most things.

Muriel

Materials:

3 balls of light worsted (DK/8-ply) silk/merino yarn; 50g/135yd/150m

Needles:

4mm (US 6, UK 8) knitting needles

Size:

Circumference: 47in (119cm), height: 8½in (21cm)

Tension:

22 sts x 30 rows = 4in (10cm) square using 4mm (US 6, UK 8) needles

Instructions:

Cast on 56 sts.

Row 1 (RS): k5, p to last 5 sts, k5.

Row 2: knit.

Row 3: k5, *p2, (k2, p2) twice, k8, rep from * once more, p2, (k2, p2) twice, k5.

Row 4: k5, *k2, (p2, k2) twice, p8, rep from * once more, k2, (p2, k2) twice, k5.

Row 5: as row 1.

Row 6: as row 2.

Row 7: as row 3.

Row 8: as row 4.

Row 9: as row 3.

Row 10: as row 4.

Row 11: k5, *p2, T3F, T3B, p2, k8, rep from * once more, p2, T3F, T3B, p2, k5.

Row 12: k5, *k3, p4, k3, p8, rep from * once more, k3, p4, k3, k5.

Row 13: k5, *p3, C4B, p3, k8, rep from * once more, p3, C4B, p3, k5.

Row 14: as row 12.

Row 15: k5, *p2, T3B, T3F, p2, k8, rep from * once more, p2, T3B, T3F, p2, k5.

Row 16: as row 4.

Row 17: as row 3.

Row 18: as row 4.

Repeat the 18-row pattern another nineteen times or until work measures approximately 47in (119cm).

Cast off loosely, leaving a long yarn tail for sewing up your work.

Making up

Press snood lightly. Join cast-on and cast-off ends using mattress stitch with RS facing. Weave in all loose ends.

This snood embraces texture and cables and can be wrapped round the neck twice. It is knitted in a silky variegated yarn but would look equally good in plain colours.

Caramel

Materials:
3 balls of light worsted (DK/8-ply) baby alpaca/
superfine merino yarn in butterscotch;
50g/122yd/112m

Needles:
4.5mm (US 7, UK 7) circular knitting needle

1 stitch marker

Size:
Circumference: 47in (119cm), height: 8in (20cm)

Tension:
15 sts x 29 rows = 4in (10cm) square using
4.5mm (US 7, UK 7) needles

Instructions:
Cast on 181 sts. Place a stitch marker to denote
start of each round. Join the round, being
careful not to twist any stitches.

Round 1: k1, *yo, k2tog, rep from * to end of
round, slip stitch marker.

Rounds 2 and 3: knit.

Repeat the above 3 rounds until work measures
approximately 8in (20cm) in height.

Cast off.

Making up

Press snood lightly. Weave in all loose ends.

*This is a really simple snood for a
beginner who has mastered the basics.
It is knitted in the round and will wrap
round the neck twice. The luxury yarn
makes it lovely and soft next to the skin.*

Minty

Materials:

1 ball of fingering (4-ply) merino/silk yarn in variegated light green; 150g/656yd/600m

Needles:

4mm (US 6, UK 8) knitting needles

Size:

Circumference: 54in (137cm), height: 9½in (24cm)

Tension:

23 sts x 24 rows = 4in (10cm) square using 4mm (US 6, UK 8) needles

Instructions:

Cast on 67 sts.

Foundation row: knit each st tbl to form a neat edge.

Row 1: (RS) k2, *ssk, k2, yo, k1, yo, k2, k2tog, repeat from * to last 2 sts, k2.

Row 2: k2, purl to last 2 sts, k2.

Repeat the above 2 rows until work measures approximately 54in (137cm).

Cast off, leaving a long yarn tail for sewing up your work.

Making up

Press snood lightly. Join cast-on and cast-off ends using mattress stitch with RS facing. Weave in all loose ends.

This snood is knitted in a simple lace pattern using a lovely spring colour and a soft, luxurious yarn that drapes beautifully when worn. It is knitted on straight needles and is long enough to wrap round the neck twice.

Harlequin

Materials:

5 balls of light worsted (DK/8-ply) alpaca yarn –
2 x lilac (A), 1 x dark blue (B), 1 x mustard (C),
1 x damson (D); 50g/131yd/120m

Needles:

4.5mm (US 7, UK 7) circular knitting needles

1 stitch marker

Size:

Circumference: 26in (66cm), height: 15½in (39cm)

Tension:

21 sts x 40 rows = 4in (10cm) square using
4.5mm (US 7, UK 7) needles

Instructions:

Using yarn A cast on 132 sts. Place a stitch
marker to denote start of each round. Join the
round, being careful not to twist any stitches.

Foundation row: knit each stitch tbl to form a
neat edge.

Rows 1–4: *k2, p2, rep from * to end of round.

Row 5: *k10, inc 1, rep from * to end of round
(144 sts).

Honeycomb stitch pattern

Start pattern (omitting row 1 in the first
pattern repeat).

Round 1: knit, using yarn A.

Round 2: purl, using yarn A.

Rounds 3–8: using yarn B, *k4, sl 2, rep from
* to end of round.

Round 9: knit, using yarn A.

Round 10: purl, using yarn A.

Rounds 11–16: using yarn C, k1, *sl 2, k4 , rep
from * to last 5 sts, sl 2, k3.

Repeat the last 16 rounds using the following
colour sequence for the pattern: B, C, D, noting
that colour A is always used for the knit and
purl rows.

Continue working the 16-round pattern repeat
until the snood measures approximately 14½in
(37cm).

Next round: *k10, k2tog, rep from * to end of
round (132 sts).

Next round: purl, using yarn A.

Next 4 rounds: using yarn A, *k2, p2, rep from
* to end of round.

Cast off.

Making up

Press snood lightly. Weave in all loose ends.

*This snood is knitted in the round and
made in a beautiful alpaca yarn where
the colours blend together well.*

Adriatic

Materials:
1 ball of laceweight (2-ply) baby alpaca/silk/
cashmere/stellina mix yarn in sparkly blue;
100g/984yd/800m

Needles:
4mm (US 6, UK 8) circular knitting needle

1 stitch marker

Instructions:
Cast on 109 sts. Place a stitch marker to denote
start of each round. Join the round, being
careful not to twist any stitches.

Round 1: k1, *yo, k2tog, k2, rep from * to end.

Round 2: p1, *p2tog, yo, p2, rep from * to end.

Round 3: k3, *yo, k2tog, k2 rep from * to last
2 sts, yo, k2tog.

Round 4: p1, *yo, p2tog, p2, rep from * to end.

Round 5: k1, *k2tog, yo, k2, rep from * to end.

Round 6: p3, *yo, p2tog, p2, rep from * to last
2 sts, yo, p2tog.

Repeat the above 6 rounds until work measures
approximately 9¼in (23.5cm).

Cast off.

Making up
Press snood lightly. Weave in all loose ends.

Size:
Circumference: 27in (69cm), height: 9¼in (23.5cm)

Tension:
16 sts x 17 rows = 4in (10cm) square using 4mm
(US 6, UK 8) needles

*This is a really pretty spring or
summer snood knitted in a lace
stitch to show off the sparkly
elements of the yarn. The yarn is
used double throughout and the
snood fits once round the neck.*

Blossom

Materials:

9 balls of light worsted (DK/ 8-ply) alpaca/merino yarn – 2 x smokey blue (A), 2 x dusky pink (B), 2 x gooseberry (C) and 2 x shocking pink (D); 50g/127yd/116m

Needles:

7mm (US 10.5, UK 2) knitting needles

Size:

Circumference: 59¾in (152cm), height: 10¾in (27cm)

Tension:

16 sts x 16 rows rows = 4in (10cm) square using 7mm (US 10.5, UK 2) needles

Instructions:

Note: yarn is held doubled throughout. Cast on 40 sts in yarn A.

Foundation row: knit each stitch tbl to form a neat edge.

Section A

Row 1 (RS): using yarn A, knit.

Row 2: k2, purl to last 2 sts, k2.

Join yarn B. From now on the first and last 2 sts of each row are knitted in the main colour for the section, to give a g st edge.

Rows 3–16: Keeping g st edge as set, work 14 rows from chart A over the middle 36 sts. The odd-numbered rows are worked from right to left and are knitted and the even-numbered rows are worked from left to right and are purled. The pattern is repeated three times

Key:

Chart A

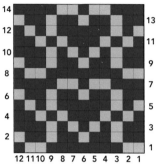

Chart B

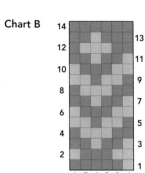

Chart C

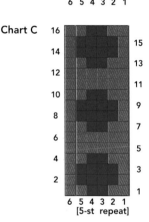

[5-st repeat]

across each row.

Fasten off yarn B.

Row 17: knit.

Row 18: k2, purl to last 2 sts, k2.

Rows 19 and 20: knit.

Fasten off yarn A.

Section B

Row 1: using yarn C, knit.

Row 2: using yarn C, k2, purl to last 2 sts, k2.

Join yarn B.

Rows 3–16: keeping g st edge as set, work 14 rows from chart B over the middle 36 sts. The pattern is repeated six times across each row.

Fasten off yarn B.

Row 17: using yarn C, knit.

Row 18: using yarn C, k2, purl to last 2 sts, k2.

Rows 19 and 20: using yarn C, knit.

Fasten off yarn C.

Section C

Row 1: using yarn D, knit.

Row 2: using yarn D, k2, purl to last 2 sts, k2.

Join yarn A.

Rows 3–18: keeping g st edge as set, work 16 rows from chart C over the middle 36 sts. The pattern repeat (marked by green borders) is worked seven times across each row. The last st is worked in D.

Fasten off yarn A.

Row 19: using yarn D, knit.

Row 20: using yarn D, k2, purl to last 2 sts, k2.

Rows 21 and 22: using yarn D, knit.

Fasten off yarn D.

Repeat sections A, B and C another three times.

Cast off, leaving a long yarn tail for sewing up your work.

Making up
Press snood lightly. Join cast-on and cast-off edges using mattress stitch with RS facing. Weave in all loose ends.

This is a fun snood to make and you can have a great time mixing and matching colours. The project uses a variety of Fair Isle designs.

Foxy Boxy

Materials:

4 x 50g balls of light worsted (DK/8-ply) superfine alpaca yarn in cream; 50g/131yd/120m

Needles:

8mm (US 11, UK 0) knitting needles

Size:

Circumference: 32¼in (82cm), height 15¾in (40cm)

Tension:

11 sts x 16 rows = 4in (10cm) square using 8mm (US 11, UK 0) needles

Instructions:

Note: The yarn is used double throughout. Cast on 45 sts.

Foundation row: knit each stitch tbl to form a neat edge.

Row 1: (RS) knit.

Row 2: purl.

Row 3: k1, p3, *k5, p3, rep from * to last st, k1.

Row 4: p1, k3, *p5, k3, rep from * to last st, p1.

Row 5: k1, *yfwd, k3tog, yfwd, k5, rep from * to last 4 sts, yfwd, k3tog, yfwd, k1.

Rows 6–8: work in st st, starting with a purl row.

Row 9: k5, *p3, k5, rep from * to end.

Row 10: p5, *k3, p5, rep from * to end.

Row 11: k5, *yfwd, k3tog, yfwd, k5, rep from * to end.

Row 12: purl.

Rep these 12 rows until work measures approximately 32¼in (82cm).

Cast off, leaving a long yarn tail for sewing up your work.

Making up

Press snood lightly. Join cast-on and cast-off ends using mattress stitch with RS facing. Weave in all loose ends.

This is a very snuggly snood made from a gorgeous alpaca yarn that is really soft. Holding the yarn double gives it a really chunky feel and the simple lace pattern adds texture and interest.

Purple Mist

Materials:
1 ball of light worsted (DK/8-ply) merino yarn in variegated purple/lilac; 100g/251yd/230m

Needles:
5.5mm (US 9, UK 5) knitting needles

Size:
Circumference: 24in (61cm), height: 8¼in (21cm)

Tension:
19 sts x 24 rows = 4in (10cm) square using 5.5mm (US 9, UK 5) needles

Instructions:
Cast on 41 sts.

Foundation row: knit all sts tbl to form a neat edge.

Row 1: k3, p2, * k1, p1, k1, p4, repeat from * to the last 8 sts, k1, p1, k1, p2, k3.

Row 2: k3, k2, * p1, k1, p1, k4, repeat from * to the last 8 sts, p1, k1, p1, k5.

Row 3: k3, p2, * kfbf, p1, kfbf, p4, rep from * to the last 8 sts, kfbf, p1, kfbf, p2, k3.

Row 4: k3, k2, *p3tog, k1, p3tog, k4, rep from * to the last 8 sts, p3tog, k1, p3tog, k5.

Repeat rows 1–4 until work measures approximately 24in (61cm).

Cast off, leaving a long yarn tail for sewing up your work.

Making up
Press snood lightly. Join cast-on and cast-off ends using mattress stitch with RS facing. Weave in all loose ends.

This is a very simple little textured snood that only uses one ball of a lovely variegated yarn.

Ophelia

Materials:
1 ball of laceweight (2-ply) alpaca/silk yarn
in rust; 100g/874yd/800m

Needles:
3.5mm (US 4, UK 10) knitting needles

Size:
Circumference: 26in (66cm),
height: 18½in (47cm)

Tension:
20 sts x 31 rows = 4in (10cm) square using
3.5mm (US 4, UK 10) needles

Instructions:
Cast on 104 sts.

Foundation row: knit each st tbl to form a
neat edge.

Row 1: (RS) knit.

Row 2 and every alternate row: purl.

Row 3: knit.

Row 5: *k4, k2tog, yfwd, k1, yfwd, sl 1, k1, psso,
k4; rep from * to end.

Row 7: *k3, k2tog, yfwd, k3, yfwd, sl 1, k1, psso,
k3; rep from * to end.

Row 9: *k2, (k2tog, yfwd) twice, k1, (yfwd, sl 1,
k1, psso) twice, k2; rep from * to end.

Row 11: *k1, (k2tog, yfwd) twice, k3, (yfwd, sl 1,
k1, psso) twice, k1; rep from * to end.

Row 13: *(k2tog, yfwd) three times, k1, (yfwd,
sl 1, k1, psso) three times; rep from * to end.

Row 14: purl.

Repeat these 14 rows until work measures
approximately 26in (66cm) ending with row 14.

Cast off, leaving a long yarn tail for sewing up
your work.

Making up
Press snood lightly. Join cast-off and cast-on
ends with RS facing using mattress stitch.
Weave in all loose ends.

*Choose your favourite colour to knit
this light and pretty snood, which
has a delicate lace design.*

Agincourt

Materials:

2 balls of fingering (4-ply) silk/wool yarn in variegated lilac; 50g/246yd/225m

Needles:

4mm (US 6, UK 8) knitting needles

Size:

Circumference: 47¼in (120cm), height: 10¾in (25cm)

Tension:

25 sts x 22 rows = 4in (10cm) square using 4mm (US 6, UK 8) needles

Instructions:

Cast on 68 sts.

Foundation row: knit all sts tbl to form a neat edge.

Row 1: k2, *kfbf, k3tog, rep from * to last 2 sts, k2.

Row 2: purl.

Row 3: k2, *k3tog, kfbf, rep from * to last 2 sts, k2.

Row 4: purl.

Repeat rows 1–4 until work measures approximately 47¼in (120cm).

Cast off, leaving a long yarn tail for sewing up your work.

Making up

Press snood lightly. Join cast-on and cast-off edges using mattress stitch with RS facing. Weave in all loose ends.

This is a really practical snood knitted in a simple lace pattern. It is worn by twisting it round the neck twice. The mixture of silk and wool give it a luxurious feel that is lovely to wear.

Abbreviations

beg	beginning
C2B	(cross 2 back) slip next st onto cable needle and hold at back of work, knit next st from left-hand needle, then knit st from cable needle
C4B	slip next two sts onto cable needle and hold at back, k2 from left-hand needle, k2 from cable needle
C2F	(cross 2 front) slip next st onto cable needle and hold at front of work, knit next st from left-hand needle, then knit st from cable needle
dec	decrease
DPN	double-pointed needles
g st	garter stitch: knit every row
inc	increase (by working into the front and back of the same stitch)
k	knit
KB1	knit into back of st
Kfbf	knit into the front, then back then front of the next st (2 sts increased)
ktbl	knit 1 row through back loop
k2tog	knit 2 stitches together
knitwise	as though to knit
MB	make bobble
M1	make 1, pick up the horizontal yarn between the current and the next st, and knit it through back loop
p	purl
p2tog	purl 2 stitches together
PM	place marker
psso	pass slipped stitch over
rem	remaining
rep	repeat
RS	right side/s
sk2po	slip one st, knit 2 stitches together, pass slipped st over the knitted st
sl	slip, usually slip 1 stitch
ssk	slip 1 st knitwise, slip next st knitwise, insert left needle into front of both sts, knit together through back loop
st(s)	stitch(es)
st st	stockinette stitch (UK stocking stitch); alternate knit and purl rows (unless directed otherwise, always start with a knit row)
tbl	through back loop
T2B	(Twist 2 Back) slip next st onto cable needle and hold at back of work, knit next st from left-hand needle, then purl st from cable needle
T3B	(Twist 3 Back) slip next st onto cable needle and hold at back of work, knit 2, then purl st from cable needle
T2BW	(Twist 2 Back on Wrong side) slip next st onto cable needle and hold at back (right side) of work, knit next st from left-hand needle, then purl st from cable needle
T3F	(Twist 3 Front) slip next 2 sts onto cable needle and hold at front of work, purl 1 then knit 2 from cable needle
T2FW	(Twist 2 Front on Wrong side) slip next st onto cable needle and hold at front (wrong side) of work, purl next st from left-hand needle, then knit st from cable needle
WS	wrong side/s
yrn	wrap yarn round needle to create an extra stitch (this makes up for the stitch you lose when you knit 2 together)
yfrn	yarn forward and over needle
yfwd	yarn forward
yo	yarn over
*	repeat the instructions following the * as many times as specified